Wicker

The Quarrelsome Celts and the Rapacious Romans

Catrin Stevens

Illustrated by Graham Howells

Gomer

First published in Welsh in 2014 by
Gomer Press, Llandysul, Ceredigion SA44 4JL
under the title *Y Celtiaid Cynhennus a'r Rhufeiniaid Rhyfygus*

ISBN 978 1 84851 828 5

This book is published with the financial support of the Welsh Books Council.

Printed and bound in Wales at Gomer Press, Llandysul, Ceredigion
Wasg Gomer, Llandysul, Ceredigion SA44 4JL

CONTENTS

INTRODUCTION

Everyone knows that History can be really horrible and that historians can be quite horrendous. But nothing brings out the worst in historians more than the history of the Quarrelsome Celts. If you want to see historians at loggerheads and bickering (what an exciting prospect!) creep up behind them and shout 'QUARRELSOME CELTS'. They'll jump out of their skins and begin arguing and quarrelling nastily.

Yes, the Quarrelsome Celts make historians quarrelsome too. Which of these historians is right? Or are you hopelessly confused?

Of course, you can use one of these arguments to avoid doing any homework on the Celts.

Oh yes, the Celts pose a HUGE HISTORICAL PROBLEM.

Well, WE'VE DECIDED – because if they didn't exist there wouldn't be a book about them, would there? So there we are and here we go!

Fussy Facts: Are they Tissues (Atishoo!) of Lies?

The terrible truth is that it is very difficult to find out what kind of people the Quarrelsome Celts really were, because they didn't write anything down on paper about themselves. Horrid historians have to depend upon the descriptions of them by their enemies, the Rapacious Romans and even worse, the Ghastly Greeks. How would your worst enemy describe you, we wonder? (No, please don't answer that question – it beggars belief!)

This is what the appalling historian, Diodorus **Sic**ulus, had to say about the Celts after he'd bumped into them (his name is enough to make you sick!):

They are terrifying to look at and their voices are deep and harsh. Also, they like to talk in superlatives, praising themselves and making small of everyone else. They also boast and threaten and they are fond of pompous language.

Was Siculus a loony liar? He certainly didn't like the Celts, did he?

And Strabo, another ghastly Greek historian, didn't have a good word for them either:

The Celts love and adore war; they're enthusiastic and very ready to fight.

It would be much better if you read everything about them in this horrible history first, and then you can decide for yourself whether these facts about the Celts are true or not. YOU DECIDE!

On the other hand, horrid historians don't have to worry about the Rapacious Romans. They had lots of their own happy historians to write their horrible history – to describe every success and to praise their awesome achievements to the hilt. Of course they never mention anything that went wrong. And so, EVERYONE knows about their evil empire, their jammy generals and their wondrous warriors. Your teachers will probably love this horrid history and will ask you stupid questions such as these about them.

Try to answer wisely.

Why do we say that the Romans were rapacious?

Because they were good at rapping, Sir?*

Why did the Romans wear sheep's wool between their toes?

Because there was no room for a whole sheep Miss?

Excellent, but there's room for improvement, so let's start with:

* Every idiot knows that rapacious has nothing to do with rapping. It means greedy of course.

A TEDIOUS TIMELINE FOR THE QUARRELSOME CELTS AND THE RAPACIOUS ROMANS

(Another wacky warning before starting. This timeline says that certain events took place BC (Before Christ) and AD (Anno Domini – After Christ). This is absolutely stupid because the Quarrelsome Celts and Rapacious Romans never used these terms themselves. But there we are – horrible History is always horribly stupid!)

64,000,000 years ago
The dinosaurs die out once and for all, Amen (but everyone knows that there's one hiding under your bed – Ooo! Ooo!)

Peepo, is it safe to come out now please?

225,000 years ago
The first men to live in Wales. (There were women living here as well of course, or there wouldn't be any children and no-one to do all the hard work!)

About 4500 BC onwards
Beginning to farm the land instead of depending on hunting only. Now, you could feast on bread AND venison. (Yum yum!)

About 3500–1200 BC

Building stone circles and cromlechs such as Pentre Ifan (who was Ifan and where was his *pentre* (village)?) in Pembrokeshire, and Barclodiad y Gawres (the Giantess's Apronful) in Anglesey. Silly men from the Preseli Hills carry 82 blue stones weighing 4 tons (c. 4000 bags of sugar) each, 240 miles over land and sea to Stonehenge in south west England.

Sorry, boys, this colour blue doesn't match. You'll have to take these stones back!

About 2500–700 BC

The Bronze Age – using copper and bronze to make tools and equipment of all kinds. Copper mined on Orme's Head, near Llandudno.

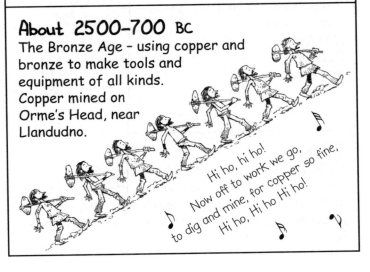

Hi ho, hi ho!
Now off to work we go,
to dig and mine, for copper so fine,
Hi ho, Hi ho Hi ho!

About 800 BC–about AD 100

The Iron Age – the Age of the Quarrelsome Celts.
Building hillforts and living in round houses.

About 650 BC

The Celts throw iron goods into the lake at Llyn
Fawr, Cwm Rhondda. What a waste!

That's it!
No more ironing
shirts for my
husband!

About 300 BC–AD 100

Throwing more valuable goods into
another lake –
Llyn Cerrig
Bach on
Anglesey.

Now where on earth
(or in water) did I
throw that sword?

55 BC

10,000 Romans, under the command of General
Julius Caesar, cross the channel into Britain to
sort out the Celts of the south-east. But the
rough weather drives them back to Gaul (or France)
(Bye Bye Baby!).

54 BC

Julius Caesar returns, with 25,000 soldiers this time (Help!). But a huge storm wrecks his ships and a rebellion in Gaul forces him to return there. (Hurray and thanks Gauls. Well, they were Celtic cousins, after all.)

AD 43 – about AD 410

The Age of the Rapacious Romans.

AD 43

Emperor Claudius (the Roman boss) orders his general, Aulus Plautius, to attack Britain. Here they come – there's nowhere to escape from the Romans now!

AD 43–51

Caradog the Celt, king of the Catuvellauni tribe in southern England, leads a guerrilla rebellion against the Romans, but is defeated in battle in AD 51. (Read more about this cool Celt on page 71.)

No, no, this is a **guerrilla**, not a **gorilla**, rebellion!

AD 52–58

The Silures tribe in south-east Wales fight against the Romans. In the beginning the Silures are successful and they defeat a legion of Roman soldiers. But then they begin to lose the day (how very, very sad!).

AD 61

A clever Roman general, Gaius Suetonius Paulinus (known as Sweaty Pole to the Celts), and his amazing army attack the Celtic druids on Anglesey. There's a massive massacre, as good as any epic Hollywood film.

BUT while he's fiddling around on Anglesey, the Iceni tribe, led by Queen Boudica, revolts in the east. Paulinus leaves Anglesey in a hurry. After a fierce battle Boudica is defeated and her rebellion comes to an end. Fearsome Boudica no longer strikes fear into the hearts of all Romans. (Read all about her on pages 65–67.)

AD 78

General Sextus Julius Frontinus (he liked to be at the front!) tries to finish the task of conquering Wales – and he begins with the Silures in the south-east.

AD 75–78

The Romans build several forts around Wales, e.g. Isca Silurum (Caerleon), Moridunum (Carmarthen) and Segontium (Caernarfon).

October AD 78

General Gnaeus Julius Agricola continues Frontius's work and attacks the Ordovices tribe in the north. Then, he proceeds to Anglesey, where there are still some dreadful druids trying to challenge the might of the Rapacious Romans. But they're defeated once and for all (until they are resurrected in modern eisteddfodau!).

AD 122

Emperor Hadrian builds a wall, 73 miles long, from Newcastle to Carlisle in northern England. Soldiers are moved from Caerleon to freeze on a wall in the far north.

Where's Hadrian's Wall?

Probably at the bottom of his garden. (Ha ha!)

AD 214

Emperor Caracalla proclaims that every free man and woman in the Roman Empire can call themselves Roman Citizens. (Wow! What an honour!)

AD 383

Magnus Maximus (Macsen Wledig to the Welsh) is promoted Roman Emperor in Britain by his own army. Dear old Macsen dreams of falling in love with lovely Helen of Caernarfon – the most beautiful woman in the whole world. (That's no surprise. What else would you expect from a Cofi from Caernarfon?) [Read all about it on p. 126]

AD 400-410

The Roman Army leaves Britain and returns to Italy. (Goodbye and good riddance?) But once they're gone, Irish from Ireland and Angles and Saxons from Europe begin to attack Britain from all sides – west, east and south. It's another nightmare!

Help, Romans! Please come back. All is forgiven.

A QUIRKY QUIZ BEFORE COMMENCING – ABOUT THE QUARRELSOME CELTS

Yes, let's begin at the beginning (how clever!) with the Quarrelsome Celts and forget about the Rapacious Romans for now. Give yourself a mark for every correct answer (very, very clever).

1. *Why were the Celts so Quarrelsome?*
(a) Quarrelsome?! Quarrelsome?! They weren't quarrelsome at all! DON'T be so cheeky!

(b) Because they were divided into tribes and one tribe would try to steal another tribe's land and cattle.
(c) Because they enjoyed bickering and quarrelling among themselves. Remember that the Celts are your great, great, great . . . grandmothers and grandfathers – if you're Welsh!

2. *What is the correct name for the people who lived in Wales during the Iron Age?*
(a) The Ironers.
(b) The Celts (but nothing to do with Celtic football team in Scotland).
(c) The Britons or Brythoniaid (but not the Brythoniaid Male Voice Choir from Blaenau Ffestiniog of course).

3. *Why did they live on top of hills?*
(a) So that they would be safer when an enemy attacked.
(b) Because they liked to freeze there in the winter cold.
(c) To enjoy the vast views.

4. *Who or what did the Celts worship?*
(a) Brilliant Welsh rugby and football players.
(b) Any film star from Wales.
(c) All kinds of different gods from the world around them.

AWESOME ANSWERS

1b: Several terrifying Celtic tribes competed for land and stole one another's cattle and goods, so they were very quarrelsome. In Wales there were four main tribes: the **Demetae** in the south-west, the **Silures** in the south-east, the **Deceangli** in the north-west and the **Ordovices** in north-west and mid Wales. That's four excellent regional rugby teams (instead of the Ospreys, the Scarlets . . .).

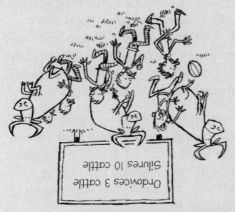

Ordovices 3 cattle
Silures 10 cattle

2b or **c?** We haven't a clue, but definitely not the Ironers, because films such as *Iron Man* hadn't appeared yet. In Europe they called similar tribes Keltoi (Celts) but in Britain perhaps the correct name was Britons or Brythoniaid. Very confusing. But does anyone care?

3a: Once again we're not sure, because a hill fort would have been a very silly place to live when there weren't any enemies around. It would make more sense to live down in the valley to farm the fertile land there. Another puzzle about the Celts, and about which historians and archaeologists quarrel all the time.

4c: Unlike Welsh people today they didn't worship rugby players and film stars from Hollywood. They much preferred worshipping a tree, a river or a well (well, well!).

THE QUARRELSOME CELTS AND THEIR WONDERFUL WARRIORS

With so many enemies – every other Celtic tribe, the Romans and then the Irish – it's not surprising that the Celts were such wonderful warriors.

Would you like to be a Wonderful Warrior? If so, you must know everything about the latest warrior fashions:

✠ You won't need to buy an expensive suit of armour – just use your birthday suit! Some Celts fought naked (or *porcyn* as the Demetae of south-west Wales would have said). The sight of your Celtic body will probably frighten your enemy senseless. If you don't fancy going naked into battle (coward!) you could wear colourful trousers and a cloak instead.

✠ But you must wear an iron helmet on your head. Make sure there's a sculpture of a wild boar on top of the helmet (the latest fashion). It will make you look taller and it will help frighten the enemy (unless he's a Celt too, of course, and wearing an even more horrendous helmet).

✠ Wear a torque around your neck – it will look nice but will be absolutely useless as protection if you're stabbed in the neck. (Arghh!)

✠ Carry a large oval wooden shield (to hide dubious bits of your body).

✠ You will need a strong iron sword to stab the enemy in his stomach, his head, his arm — anywhere will do — OR a long spear to hurl at the enemy to kill him.

✠ And to complete the loathsome look get a tasty tattoo.

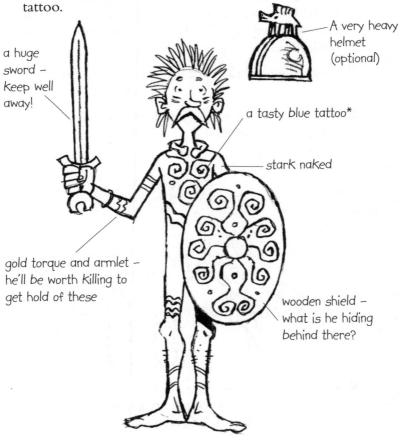

A very heavy helmet (optional)

a huge sword – keep well away!

a tasty blue tattoo*

stark naked

gold torque and armlet – he'll be worth killing to get hold of these

wooden shield – what is he hiding behind there?

* One fantastic fact about wearing a woad tattoo to go into battle: believe it or not, woad works as an antiseptic. And so, if a warrior was injured the woad would help him to get better more quickly. What very, very clever Celts!

To make a tasty tattoo

(not by visiting a tattoo parlour in Swansea):

1. Gather some woad plants and dry the leaves by hanging them upside down for about a year (don't use your hairdryer for this!). Let's hope your enemy has enough time and patience to wait for you to do this.

2. Once the leaves are dry, grind them into fine powder.

3. Make this into a paste by adding water or pee. (O.K. you might stink, but it will help to keep the enemy at bay!)

I asked for tattoos not *tatws* (potatoes)!

4. Paint the woad dye onto your body in lovely patterns of spirals and swirls. Ask a friend to paint your back or there'll be a mess!

5. Now, you're ready to go into battle – your tasty tattoo will terrify the most terrifying enemy. (Let's hope so, anyway.)

How to fight – in the Celtic style

As a wonderful warrior you will now be ready to fight in the Celtic style. That Rapacious Roman, Julius Caesar, gives us the best description of this style:

The Celts fight from war chariots drawn by horses. They drive the chariots all over the battlefield hurling javelins at the enemy. The terror inspired by the horses and the noise of the wheels are sufficient to throw their opponents' ranks into disorder. The Celtic warrior can run along the chariot pole, stand on the yoke, and get back into the chariot as quick as lightning. The warriors will practise driving their horses every day until they are experts at it and they can drive their horses at a gallop, then stop and turn them around in a minute.

But the main tactic was to frighten and terrify the enemy by looking scary in a huge helmet, with blue tattoos, and by making a horrible din, with the chariot wheels clanging and a trumpet sounding loudly. It was enough to make the enemy's hair stand on end!

Unfortunately, however, we've got to admit that, in fact, the Quarrelsome Celts were pretty useless warriors on the battlefield. Their battles were shambolic because of all the blood curdling screaming and shouting.

I'm off – order and organisation or not. I've got an appointment at the hairdresser's.

Off with their Heads

Quarrelsome Celtic warriors had one very horrible habit. When they chanced upon a headstrong enemy they cut off his head (after killing him of course). Then they would tie the head to their horse's saddle and show it off to all their friends to prove what wonderful warriors they were.

The tribal chiefs would go head to head to capture the best heads. (They could have played a good game of heads or tails with these, couldn't they?!)

I've got the best heads. Ta-ra-ra-ra-ra! I've got a headstrong one, a big-head and a hot head!

I'm gutted, I've collected the wrong ends!

When they arrived home they would soak these heady heads in cedar oil and then:

 either store them in a chest in their homes to show friends who called for a chat and a cuppa (they wouldn't remain friends for long in that stink!)

 or hang them out to dry in front of their homes like Christmas decorations today, so that everyone could see what wonderful warriors they were.

It all came to a head when only the skulls were left – swaying and blowing beautifully in the wind.

Am-a-zing

And when they held a nice little birthday party to celebrate the custom of head hunting, someone was bound to tell the tiresome tale from the Mabinogion about a great Celtic giant called Bendigeidfran and his am-a-zing head. Here's a chapter from the story.

> The story so far:
> Bendigeidfran the giant and an army of Welshmen had gone over to Ireland to rescue Branwen, the giant's sister, from her cruel husband, Matholwch, King of Ireland.

> But war broke out between the Welsh and the Irish, and everyone, except for seven of the warriors and Branwen, was killed.

> Even giant Bendigeidfran was seriously injured in his shoulder by a poisoned dart.

And now – Chapter 2 of the tiresome tale:

> I'm dying boys. Cut off my head and take it back to Britain. But don't forget this piece of advice . . .

> Bendigeidfran – you're doing my head in. I can't cut your head off unless you shut up!

A PITIFUL POSTSCRIPT

And where were the women while the men were out
fighting and killing, maiming and murdering? No, not
at home cooking Celtic cockles or British *bara brith*,
but out on the battlefield itself. They loved seeing
blood flow and heads roll. Read more about these
woeful women (if you have the guts) on pages 63–70.

BEYOND BELIEF! THE QUARRELSOME CELTS AND THEIR RELIGION

They say that you can't really understand the Quarrelsome Celts without knowing about their religion. But it's difficult to believe what the Celts believed. So, what can we believe? Believe you me, you'll have a job to decide whether these facts are **TRUE** or **FALSE**.

(i) The Celts thought that the number two was a sacred number. They could only count up to two (one, two). Remember the old Celtic verse:

Two little Celts going to the wood,
Two little Celts up to no good . . .

TRUE or **FALSE**?

(ii) The Celts had lots of different gods. They worshipped trees, rivers, animals, birds and many other things from the natural world (even rats and sheep (ba–a–a!).

TRUE or **FALSE**?

(iii) The Celts believed that people who died could be re-born (the world would be very full!) and that dead warriors who were thrown into a magic cauldron during a battle would come back alive. Surprise, surprise!

TRUE or **FALSE**?

(iv) The Celts believed that Christmas trees were very lucky. They would decorate them with bright lights and put a druid to sparkle on the top.

TRUE or **FALSE**?

(v) The Celts loved to eat a tart filled with mistletoe (a parasitic plant with white berries) for breakfast, lunch, tea and supper.

Not another mistletoe tart, Mum. Why can't we have a cherry or gooseberry one instead, please?

Don't be daft. The Romans haven't brought those fruits to Wales yet.

TRUE or **FALSE**?

(vi) When there was an emergency – such as when lurid legions of Rapacious Romans were about to attack them – the Celts would run to the nearest lake and throw all kinds of valuable metal objects into it. They'd throw swords or shields (how silly was that? – how could they possibly fight without them?); cauldrons (but how could they make Celtic *cawl* without them?) and horses' gear. (Gee, how stupid!)

TRUE or **FALSE**?

And of course: 'Three tries for a Welshman (and a Welshwoman)'.

And on top of all that they liked to use the shape of a triskel, (three-skel) in their beautiful art work.

(ii) **Very TRUE.** The horse goddess was called Epona; Lieu was the god of light; Taranis was the god of thunder and lightning (*taran* is thunder in Welsh) and the horned god, called Cern-unnos, was one of the most popular gods.

> No, no, get off my corn – I'm not Corn-unnos. Ouch!

(iii) **Truly TRUE.** The Mabinogion tales tell the story of a magical rebirth cauldron (though this is a legend of course, so it can't be trusted). When the Welsh were fighting the Irish in Ireland to try to rescue Branwen, the Irish would throw their dead warriors into the magic cauldron of rebirth. But Efnisien, Branwen's brutal half-brother, jumped into the cauldron and tore it in half. (What a nasty piece of work – spoiling all the fun!)

(iv) **FALSE.** No-one celebrated Christmas or cared whether there was room at the inn in Bethlehem in Celtic times. Their favourite trees were oak trees (*derw* in Welsh) and perhaps this is how the druids (*derwyddon*) got their name.

(v) **FALSE** – Mistletoe berries are very, very poisonous. If the Celts ate them they would have an awful stomach ache or diarrhoea (ych-a-fii).

So why did the daft druids go out to collect mistletoe? Perhaps they wanted to kiss and cuddle delightful druidesses underneath it.

33

I think the Celts were crackers, throwing valuable items like these into water.

So do I. I just hope all this money brings me good luck!

(vi) **TRUE**. Oh yes it is! Am-a-zing collections of such objects have been found in lakes in Wales – in Llyn Fawr in Cwm Rhondda and Llyn Cerrig Bach on Anglesey. Sometimes the objects that have been found have been broken deliberately. In Llyn Cerrig Bach one sword had been bent in half – so that no-one else could use it. How spiteful was that? These were presents and offerings to the gods. The Celts believed that the gods would refuse to help them to win battles, to kill enemies or to harvest their crops unless they received sacrifices of valuable objects like these.

ΤΗΕ FANΤΑSΤΙC FESΤΙVALS OF ΤΗΕ QUARRELSOME CELΤS

If you lived in Celtic times you could have enjoyed not just **THREE** school holidays a year to go to Llangrannog and Disneyland – you would have had **FOUR**. Here is their captivating calendar:

FEBRUARY 1: to celebrate the end of winter and the beginning of summer. (How stupid – in such cold weather!) The Irish Celts called this fantastic festival – Imbolc. A great occasion to eat and drink as much as you could.

MAY 1: Mayday, to celebrate summer, when the cattle could be driven out onto the open fields to graze. Thank goodness – fewer cowpats around the house (PONG!). This fantastic festival was called Beltane after the sun god – Belenos. Another occasion to eat and drink to excess!

On May Eve (the night before Mayday) they would light huge bonfires and drive the cattle between them. For some reason they thought this would cure and purify the cattle from any diseases.

Ouch! My feet are burning. If I didn't have foot and mouth disease before, I'll definitely have it now!

AUGUST 1: A trip to the National Eisteddfod? No way! A fantastic festival to celebrate the harvest and to thank Lleu (or Lughnasadh), the god of light, for ensuring that the crops had ripened once again this year. Another opportunity for a feast of food and drink.

Halloween or October 31 and November 1:

The beginning of winter and of the Celtic year. It was called Samhain and it was another chance to gorge and drink excessively. To celebrate Halloween they built bonfires again, and this time the Celts themselves ran back and fore through the smoke and ashes, following the sun's orbit. (Fancy a smoked Celt?) Some of them would mark a stone with a cross and throw it into the fire.

Then, they'd come back in the morning to look for it. If they found it, this brought them good luck (an opportunity to capture a head or two perhaps – but keep your head!). But if not, they would have very, very bad luck (fall head-first into a cowpat at least!).

The Celts thought that at Halloween the boundary between life and death disappeared. Ghastly ghosts such as the *Hwch Ddu Gota* (the short-tailed black sow – ych-a-fi!) and the Bogeyman (boo!) lurked round every corner, ready to jump out suddenly to frighten the living daylights out of you. (Don't look round now – there's a *Bwci Bo* coming!)

Boo! Boo!

The Wicked Wickerman

Halloween was a nerve-racking night for every crazy Celtic criminal or prisoner. This was when they would be punished and sacrificed alive inside the wicked wickerman! The Celts would make a huge effigy from basket or wickerwork to celebrate this occasion. Then, they would gather up all the nasty criminals and prisoners to fill it. If there weren't enough thieves and murderers you could throw in a badger or a fox or two too.

Now fill in this invitation (if you're not too much of a coward) and come and enjoy this dramatic and exciting event in the captivating Celtic calendar.

The crazy Celtic Druids would like to invite:
(write your name here please)

_____

TO THE FUNKY
WICKED WICKERMAN FESTIVAL

on Halloween (the fire will be lit at midnight).
Bring your favourite criminals and prisoners to be burned alive.
We extend a (very) warm welcome to everyone.*

This isn't fair.
All I did was burn
the toast!

* One fiery warning – the only ones to mention this curious custom were the Rapacious Roman, Julius Caesar, and the gruesome Greek, Strabo, and we all know what they thought of their enemies, the Celts – so where's that pinch of salt? When the film, _The Wicker Man_, (you'll never guess what it was about!) was screened in 1974, the audience was too frightened to go home from the cinema at the end! (What cowardly custards!)

On November 1 there would be another massive massacre, when all the animals that weren't going to be kept alive through the winter would be butchered. The Welsh name for this slaughtering was *tachweddu* and so we have the name of the month *Tachwedd* for November. (I bet even your woeful Welsh teachers don't know this.)

When lots of animals had been slaughtered, the Quarrelsome Celts invited their best friends to share a glorious meaty feast with them. And they would throw all the entrails (brains, liver, heart, stomach, lungs, intestines – and any other ych-a-fi pieces), not to the dogs, but to the poor poor.

A Day in the Life of a Dozy Druid

If there had been Sunday magazines in the year AD 79 this kind of story would probably have appeared on their pages.

This week come with us to Anglesey to meet Derwyn the dozy druid and to find out how he's going to spend his day.

I get up at six o'clock, as dawn breaks. Today is a very, very IMPORTANT day for every dramatic druid. So, there's no time for a bath – I only bathe twice a year anyway (what's that stink?). I put on my long white robe, sandals on my feet and a ring of laurel leaves around my head. I can't remember when I last saw myself in a mirror. I only take a quick peek at myself sometimes in a pool of water (peekaboo – what a sight!). I eat a breakfast of wheaten bread full of bits of grit (CRUNCH!). No wonder I've got hardly any teeth left.

Dash! I can't get my teeth into anything now!

I go straight to the scintillating school for student druids. The school is chock-a-block since the Romans attacked us so cruelly in AD 60. Suddenly, all the young people in the country want to join the dozy druids of Anglesey. They've probably heard that the druids don't have to fight battles, and don't have to pay taxes either.

Why do you think I joined up? Because I'm a cowardly miser of course!

In school I have to teach the student druids how to exercise their memories so that they can remember everything. We druids never write anything down – not like the Rapacious Romans. I think reading and writing are a waste of time. (Don't show this sentence to your tiresome teachers!) Instead, we exercise our memories constantly by repeating verses or by counting things in threes. This is a dainty ditty I composed to help the dozy druids exercise their memories and remember everything. Isn't it lucky I can remember it? (What was it again?)

> Remember to practise remembering
> Remember to enjoy the training,
> When eating and drinking,
> Sacrificing and sleeping
> AND on the loo – keep on trying!

(Come on! I'm a dozy druid not a brainy bard).
It takes twenty years for a baby druid to become a fully-fledged, grown-up druid.

Back you go to school – you've only been a pupil here for 19½ years!

After a miserable hour in the scintillating school I hurry over to the groovy grove in the trees to see what the Archdruid wants us to do today. I hope he doesn't want us to harvest mistletoe again. I've had more than enough of climbing trees to cut the mistletoe down from the oak trees with a golden *sickle* (how *sickening*!) so that it falls into a white cloth. For some reason I'm always up the wrong tree. The Archdruid has threatened to make me eat the mistletoe if this happens once more (stomach ache – diarrhoea – death – no thanks!).

Ooops, I'm barking up the wrong tree – AGAIN!

But no, thank goodness, today's tragic task is to make a sacrifice. I really enjoy sacrificing pathetic prisoners or stupid slaves. And it's a good idea to give them some mistletoe berries to eat beforehand. This ensures they're in such terrible pain they don't even feel the sting of the spear.

I'm in charge of the sacrifice today (WOW!) and the petrified offering is ready. I hold the spear up high and throw it (WHOOSH!). Thank goodness I don't miss, or I'd be the next sacrifice. As the victim falls we watch his every movement carefully. These movements tell us, clever druids, what is going to happen in the future. Mm . . . mm . . . he's tossing and turning – does this mean that the Romans are going to attack us this afternoon? If so, you've chosen an interesting day to spend time with Derwyn, the dozy druid.

And now, to take out the entrails – (slush-slush!) – blood spurts everywhere.

Here is our sacrifice, Oh gods! Can you tell us when the next battle against the Romans will be?

I haven't got the heart to tell you, sorry!

The Archdruid stands and looks at the horrible mess and he tries to read the future (or the present) from it. He looks very, very serious. Yes, he agrees – the Rapacious Romans are due to attack at any moment NOW! Help! Help! . . . They're here . . . Help! . . .

Unfortunately, it wasn't possible to finish this interesting interview. The Rapacious Romans, led by their cruel general Agricola★ (not Coca Cola's brother), had arrived. Agri (to his friends) was determined to kill every druid on Anglesey. And how did this grotesque general succeed? He used local Celts (the treacherous traitors) to help him cross the great Menai Straits. The locals were good swimmers, or so they claimed, and of course Agri didn't care one jot whether they drowned or not. They led him and his army to the groovy golden grove where the druids were worshipping and sacrificing.

You should have told Agricola that we won at the Olympics for playing football not for swimming!

And when they arrived there was a massive massacre (**BANG! SBLAT! OUCH!**) and that was the end of the dreadful druids – forever and ever, Amen.

★ By the way, this sobering story is reported by Agricola's nephew, the horrendous historian, Cornelius Tacitus. He adored Uncle Agricola – so, once again, please don't swallow this story without plenty of Anglesey sea salt.

AN UNFORTUNATE FACT:

After killing the sacrifice, Derwyn the dozy druid had forgotten to throw his sacred spear into the lake in Llyn Cerrig Bach to please the gods and to ensure their help against the Roman enemy. And, naturally, the Celtic gods were very, very, very angry with him – you know the rest of the story.

EVERYDAY LIFE WITH THE QUARRELSOME CELTS

Who's Who

In the Quarrelsome Celtic Age everyone knew who
was who and where they fitted into their society.
NO-ONE could move up or down that social ladder.
To be honest, it was like your school today – the Head
at the top, the teachers and the assistants in the middle
and at the bottom – you, the poor pupils, who do all
the work.

This is how it worked (or didn't!):

The King and Queen –
we're the BOSSES
(don't you dare
challenge us!)

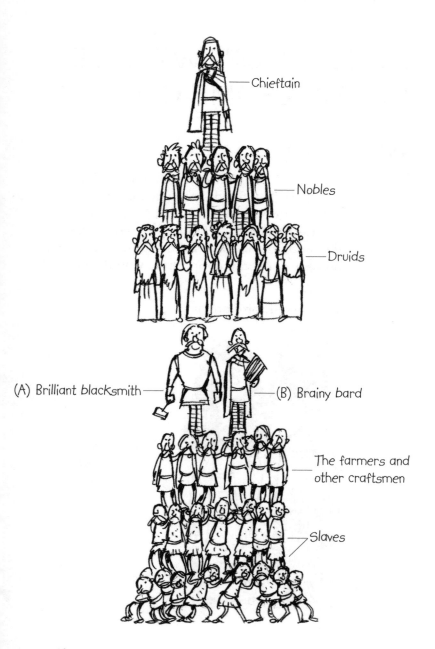

Chieftain

Nobles

Druids

(A) Brilliant blacksmith

(B) Brainy bard

The farmers and other craftsmen

Slaves

Who's Who

The King and Queen, of course,

then the Chieftains of the tribes and their families –
the middling meddling BOSSES

The rich Nobles –
the wondrous warriors
(they think THEY're important too –
they are the teeny-weeny BOSSES)

The dramatic Druids
(They should be on the same level as the Nobles
because THEY speak to the gods)

The brilliant blacksmith (A);
and the brainy bard (B):
((A) Since he's the blacksmith, working with iron
to make swords and all kinds of other objects,
it's obvious that he's a very important craftsman.
(B) As a brainy bard he's expected to compose beautiful
poems and stories about heroes, battles and hunting,
so he's very important too.

The farmers and the other craftsmen
(They do most of the hard work)

But at the bottom there is one more sad lot
and these do the worst jobs in the whole wide world:
(digging for gold in the dark underground mines or
clearing cowpats (PONG!) in the hillforts)
There are thousands of them, poor insignificant slaves
(They could be burnt alive as a sacrifice to the
gods at Halloween!)

Fantastic fact

You don't believe the Quarrelsome Celts kept pitiful slaves?

Well, think again – a slave chain, which would be used to join five slaves together by their necks, was found in Llyn Cerrig Bach on Anglesey in 1942.

The workers on the site didn't realise that the Celts had thrown this slave chain into the lake, probably as a pretty little present to keep the gods happy. The chain was so strong it was used for some time to pull vehicles out of the marsh!

Hey, that's MINE!

Good Lord! But it's been in the water for almost 2000 years!

HOMELY HOMES

If you were an estate agent, buying and selling homes in the Quarrelsome Celtic Age, this is how you would probably have gone about it.

[One clever clue: remember that your aim is to sell the house so you can boast, exaggerate and tell as many lies as you want about it . . .].

FOR SALE

CARTREF

Number 3 (the magical number) Garnedd Goch Hillfort, The land of the Ordovican Tribe, Mid Wales

Location: on top of a windy hill, lovely in bright summer sunshine (*forget the winter storms of rain and snow*), with a fantastic view over the valley below. It's well defended by ditches and earth ramparts. (*Don't mention the fact that the Deceangli tribe attacked last year and killed half the people in the hillfort.*)

Outside: Everything in this hut is sustainable. Notice the simple round shape (the latest fashion). Then, note the strong walls of oak planks with wicker woven back and fore through them and plastered with daub – an excellent way to save energy. No windows (another way to save on energy bills and of course, you won't have to clean them!)

How to make disgusting daub:
You will need – 15 tons (1,000 kilograms) of clay
              The same amount of cow dung

Method
1. Mix the clay and cow dung well. The best way is to tread in down with your feet (sludge, sludge!)
2. Then, chuck the mucky mixture at the wicker wall with all your might until it sticks like glue. If you're a bit of a wimp you can leave this disgusting task to your slaves. It will take you a month to finish the whole round house (unless it rains and it all turns into a murky mess of course).
3. When it has dried in the summer, the daub will be like a hard rock cake (but don't try to eat it!).

- Notice the remarkable roof of reeds (*Hope they don't notice there isn't a chimney and that there are all kinds of flies and mice living in pretty little nests in it*). Look too at the dramatic decoration hanging by the door. It's the skull of an enemy chief from a neighbouring tribe.

Inside: Ouch – watch your head! Too late! Your eyes and nose won't take a minute to get used to the dark and the thick smoke from the fireplace.

Two little bats hanging so high
Upside down, warm and dry;
But the frightful fumes and the heavy smoke
Make the pretty little bats cough and choke.

- Open plan living, where everyone can cook, live, sleep and play in the same room. (Sharing a room with your parents and having to suffer their snoring all night? No thank you very much!)

- Room for six (*six dwarfs perhaps*) but no toilet, so if nature calls (coo-ee!) you'll have to rush for the hedge. Unfortunately you'll have to share your hedge with everyone else in the hillfort.

- The present owners are willing to sell their furniture too – a pile of rugs and bracken for the children's beds (*watch the bed bugs*) and wooden planks and smelly animal skins for the adults (*watch out for fleas and nits*).

- For an extra cost you can have the grand fireplace and the fire itself (the Celts believed that if the fire in the hearth died, bad luck would strike them dead too – WHAM!).

Woe unto us, Woe unto us – the fire has died!

Hallelujah, Hallelujah! What good luck! I can cancel my doctor's appointment now. My cough is better already!

- There aren't any tables or chairs but there's a weaving frame and a quern (for grinding corn) for the wife (the women did all the important work – farming, looking after the animals, cooking food, making the clothes – have I made my point?).

And there we are. Your house is sure to sell in the blink of a blinking eye (BLINK!).

Let's join the fashion parade

The Quarrelsome Celts certainly knew how dress up in the latest fashions to create an impressive impression.

Incredible hair – like a horse's mane. They washed their hair in lime until it was as stiff as a poker. Then they would pull it back tightly until it stood on end and made them look like peculiar punk-rockers*

A long moustache hanging down over the mouth. Bits of food would lodge in this from time to time**

A neat little beard

A beautiful brooch to fasten the cloak

An am-a-zing amulet

A short woollen tunic

Colourful wide trousers – which they called 'braccae'****

A gold, silver or iron torque, not to strangle the wearer, but to keep evil spirits at bay (Bye bye Bogeyman!)***

Untidy long curly hair (try using straighteners, dear!)

No moustache

No beard

A colourful striped or check woollen cloak – warm in winter, cool in summer (how cool!)

Light leather shoes or sandals in summer.

A woollen dress with a girdle around the waist

Nice Notes

★ Celtic Punk-rockers

★★ Ych-a-fi –YUK!

★★★ According to Posidonius, another horrendous historian from Greece, the Celts loved jazzy jewellery.

★★★★ The Rapacious Romans had quite a shock to see the Quarrelsome Celts' trousers. They usually wore short dresses to sunbathe on the beaches of Italy. But, perhaps woollen trousers were better suited to the wind and rain of Wales, after all!

Come to the Fabulous Feast

You'll never get to know the Quarrelsome Celts properly unless you join them in a fabulous Celtic feast. Put on your glad rags and your favourite jewels and enjoy the feasting and drinking. Don't worry, there won't be any hare's meat, foul fowls or gabbling geese on the menu – the Celts weren't allowed to eat these (according to Julius Caesar – if you can believe a word he says about them).

This was their magnificent menu:

Ouch! Don't hurt your tongue when eating nettles. Follow the recipe! Ouch!

The best warrior always had the choicest piece of meat to eat. Yum! Yum!

Don't worry, a kid is a baby goat so they won't be eating you or any of the other kids in your school!

THE MAGNIFICENT MENU

Starters:
Stinging Nettle soup

Main course
Wild boar with wild garlic
or
*Goat or kid's meat and spinach
(are you kidding?)*

Pudding:
*Hazel nuts, blackberries
and sloes*

*Plenty of wine which has
NOT been watered down*

First, try to catch your wild boar (this is NOT a reference to your boring History teacher but to a wild pig!). Watch out for the wild garlic – it will make your breath stink but will keep your enemies at bay.

Enjoy! The Romans thought the Celts were daft not to water down their wine. BUT the Celts knew best! Hic!

A Recipe for Stinging Nettle Soup

Ingredients
400 grams of stingies
(or stinging nettles)
Onions, carrots and leeks to taste
1 litre of water (remember that in
Celtic times water was filthy
and full of sewage – but it'll
help to boil it first)

Method:
1. Wear thick gloves up to your elbows to gather the stingies or you will have the most awful red rash itching and prickling, stinging and tingling for hours (itch! itch!).
2. Wash the young green leaves thoroughly.
3. Melt a little bacon fat (from the wild boar) in a large cauldron and cook the leeks, the carrots and onions in it slowly. Add the nettles and the water.
4. Boil the mixture well for about half an hour over a wood fire.
5. Eat and enjoy!

A corny query about stinging nettles

Why do stinging nettles sting and tingle?
  (i) To stop animals eating them
 (ii) Because they're horrible, nasty plants

(iii) To help the Rapacious Romans to endure the cold Welsh weather. They whipped themselves with stinging nettles which would make them hop, skip and jump around with pain to keep themselves warm. (Why didn't they use a hot-water bottle?)

And after a fabulous feast of food and drink, you could play a gruesome little game with your friends before the night was out.

To play badger in a bag
You will need:
- A very angry badger
- A strong bag

- A thick stick for each player
- Between 2 and 6 players (don't have more players than this or you won't have as much fun hitting the badger)

You won't need:
- Any rules
- Or a referee

1. Go out at night to capture your badger.
2. Be careful, it can become very angry and nasty when it's cornered. I wonder why? Tie it in a strong bag.

I've had enough of this – stop badgering me!

3. And then every warrior present in the feast (not the women – they're far too sensible) can have a whale (or badger) of a time whacking and hitting the poor badger in the bag, until it begins to scream and squeal loudly and the bag rolls all over the place.

Can you call this sport? Where was the fun in it? What a horrible hobby!

PRECIOUS PORTRAIT OF A HOPELESS HERO

History teachers love and adore, and go completely bananas when they tell the truly tragic story of this hopeless hero. I hope you don't begin to cry uncontrollably when you read it or you'll spoil your priceless copy of *The Quarrelsome Celts*.

NAME: Mr Lindow II; but to be clever, English historians often call him Pete Marsh, a dodgy joke based on the fact that he was found in a peat (Pete) marsh. Ha! Ha!

They found Mrs Lindow I, Mr Lindow II's neighbour, in 1983. All that was left of her, poor thing, was a piece of her skull, one eye and a little of her hair. The police didn't realise at first that she was so old. But in fact she was 1750 years old and had lived in around AD 250. At the time the police were aware that a local woman had disappeared in 1960, and that her husband was in prison for another crime.

I'm keeping my eye on you, mate!

When they told their prisoner that they had found a woman's skull he screamed 'I confess! I confess! She's my wife! I killed her – honestly!' And he was found guilty of this murder, even though it wasn't his wife's skull at all, but old Mrs Lindow I's skull. He should have kept his mouth shut!

AÒÒRESS: Lindow Moss, Wilmslow, Cheshire (O.K., O.K., I know Wilmslow isn't in wicked Wales, but the Celts used to live in this area before the Rapacious Romans arrived). By today, the crinkly half body has been frozen and dried and is kept in a glass case in the British Museum in London, where school pupils are forced to go to see and admire it.

AGE: About 26 years old when he died, but about 1,900 years old by now.

APPEARANCE: Height: about 1.68 – 1.73 metres; weight: 60 kilograms.

A very ugly blackish-brown head and body. (I wonder how you would look if you'd been lying in peat for over 1,900 years?) Archaeologists believe they may have discovered both his legs now, too. (No, I'm not pulling your leg!)

He had a tidy beard, a moustache and sideburns (hair growing down his cheeks not out of his ears). Scientists have succeeded in making a replica of his head. He was quite good-looking!

WORK: Not a lot – he had clean, neat nails (so he couldn't have been a farmer [sorry farmers] or a coal miner could he?). He was probably one of the Celtic *crachach* (posh people).

Pretty Pete

History: We don't know a great deal about how he lived. BUT lots of people have been arguing about how he died, and why:

1. Andy Mould (what an apt name for someone who discovered a mouldy body):

On August 1st, 1984, I was loading the machine which cuts peat into small pieces when I saw something like a piece of wood. I picked it up and threw it at my friend Eddie Stack (what else are friends for!). BANG! It fell on the floor and broke in half and we saw a man's foot fall out of it! Wow – we called the police at once.

2. A detective from the Cheshire police:

I knew that something fishy was afoot at once. It was obvious that he had drowned in the peat marsh but what else had happened to the maggoty man? He had probably been murdered but the body was too old and rotten for the police to touch. So we asked for the help of:

3. A clueless archaeologist:

Well, this discovery could make me world-famous! Finding a bog-body. Before long I found the rest of the body and the arms – but no sign of legs (they must have run away!). But I didn't have a clue what had actually happened to the poor soul, so I asked for the opinion of:

4. A pathetic pathologist:

I was delighted to welcome the brill body into my shining laboratory. And here are my notes after my exciting examination:

- I noticed that he was naked except for a fox fur armband (where was his swimming costume? was the fur armband a Celtic armlet?).
- Then, I cut his stomach open. And what did I see inside? No, not curry or ice cream but some burnt toast (Celtic toasters were hopeless!) and the remains of mistletoe pollen (this is an excellent clue – check pages 31 and 41).
- I examined his head next and saw that someone had:

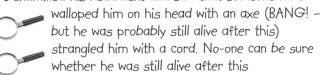

walloped him on his head with an axe (BANG! – but he was probably still alive after this)

strangled him with a cord. No-one can be sure whether he was still alive after this slit his throat (SLOOSH! and there we are – as dead as a Dodo!)

I came to the obvious conclusion that someone wanted him dead!

- And to crown it all he'd been placed head down in the bog and drowned (UGH . . . GLUG!).

After a lot of head scratching I had to agree with the detective's vile verdict that poor Pete Marsh had been murdered. But by whom and why? I didn't have a clue so I asked for the opinion of:

4. A haughty historian:

 Since I know everything there is to know about the Quarrelsome Celts I believe Mr Lindow II was tortured (that is – someone enjoyed inflicting pain on him) before he was sacrificed in a colourful religious ceremony.

By whom? The dramatic druids of course. They enjoyed performing pantomimes like this. They loved the number THREE and so this poor creature was killed in three different ways – walloped, strangled and his throat was slit. And do remember that the delightful druids threw valuable swords and shields into water to win the favour of the gods. This time they threw a body instead (SPLASH!).

Why? As a sacrifice to appease their great gods because they were so angry that the Quarrelsome Celts were being conquered by the Rapacious Romans.

When? When the Romans were attacking the Celts of course. I would like to suggest that this sacrifice was made when Paulinus was attacking the druids in Anglesey around AD 60.

And there we are – the crime neatly solved. Haughty historians always think they know all the answers, don't they?

WONDROUS CELTIC WOMEN

Woe betide you if you chance upon a wondrous Celtic woman. According to the Rapacious Romans they were even more ferocious fighters than the men, and it's easy to believe. Why not give them marks out of ten and decide which of these women you would crown as champion of the wondrous Celtic women?

Number 1: Cartimandua, queen of the Brigantes, a large Celtic tribe in northern England. She was a nasty piece of work. When Caradog the Coolest Celt was forced to flee after losing a battle against the Romans in AD 51, he decided to turn to another Celt for help. And he turned to Cartimandua. But was she his friend or the Rapacious Romans' friend? Unfortunately for poor Caradog she chose the Romans. She placed Caradog in shackles and delivered him as a prisoner to the Romans.

And the traitorous queen's treachery paid off well for her. She became very wealthy. Then she and her husband, Venutius, had a divorce and they started to fight for the lands of the Brigantes. Once more the Romans helped her. They sent a legion of soldiers to make sure that Cartimandua was victorious.

But, Venutius wouldn't surrender. In AD 69 he raised a huge army of Celtic warriors to fight against his former wife. This time the Romans couldn't come to her rescue and Cartimandua was defeated – once and for all. Serve her right – the querulous queen.

Number 2: Anglesey's awesome women. Not just one woman this time but an army of woeful women. When Paulinus, the ghastly Roman general, attacked Anglesey in AD 61, he was prepared for the dreadful druids and the fierce Celtic fighters. But who was waiting for his army on the beaches on the other side of the Menai Straits? Hundreds of fearsome women. They wore flowing black robes (swimming costumes weren't in fashion in Celtic times), their long black hair stuck out in all directions and they

Ah! Ah! Ah! Don't you dare venture across the Straits or we'll burn you to a cinder. Ah! Ah! Ah! This is our island – go away now! Ah! Ah! Ah!

brandished flaming torches! What a frightfully frightening sight! And to cap it all they were screaming and crying, threatening and cursing like banshees.

It sent shivers down every fearful Roman soldier's spine. But in spite of the deafening drama the whole thing turned into a tragedy. Paulinus persuaded his soldiers to close their eyes and attack. (Take that! (Not the pop group!) and that!) Before long all Anglesey's awesome women had been killed or they'd run away. (Though it's said that there are still some awesome women living on Anglesey. So take care the next time you cross the Menai Straits. Ah! Ah! Ah!)

Number 3: Boudica, the majestic queen of the Iceni tribe, who died in AD 61. She deserves a brilliant ballad all to herself:

> Have you heard the story of the Celtic queen,
> The wondrous Boudica,
> Who ruled the mighty Icenis
> Faraway in East Anglia?
> With long, red flowing tresses,
> She was striking to behold,
> Her voice rang out like thunder,
> And her eyes were defiant and bold.
>
> But Boudica met a cruel fate
> On the death of her husband and king,[1]
> The Roman army seized her lands
> And pillaged and burnt everything.

[1] Her husband's name was Prasutagus. This foolish man left his Kingdom, on his death, to his wife Boudica, his daughters and to the Roman Emperor. Didn't he realise that his wife didn't stand a chance against the might of the Roman Empire?

They dragged out poor Boudica,
They stripped her naked and bare,
They whipped and whipped her brutally
And ravished her daughters fair.

Now Boudica was angry and mad,
She could contain her fury no more,
She raised an army of ten thousand men
To avenge these wrongs, to be sure.
And when she reached Camulodunum[2]
She burned the town to the ground,
And any Romans who crossed her path
Were murdered. Her revenge was unbound.

And then they marched on London,
For fun and games – Whoop-ee!
A Roman historian[3] present claimed
They had quite a jamboree.
The women of London were pierced through
Like kebabs on nasty sharp spears,
Their breasts were torn from their bodies
And sewn into their mouths, poor dears.

But before you throw up or vomit
As you read this history through,
Do remember that our Superwoman,
Believed she was right and true –
From the greed of the Roman Emperor
To defend her people and land,

[2] Colchester today – a town in Essex.

[3] His name was Dio Cassius – but don't forget that the Romans were the sworn enemies of the Celts and therefore they were always prepared to say all kinds of very, very horrible things about them. He claims that about 70,000 were killed (almost enough to fill the Millenium Stadium in Cardiff) by this crazy Celtic army.

And that one day the Celts would thank her
For her brave and courageous stand.

But that evening as home she travelled
She came to a sticky end,
Paulinus's[4] army beat the Celts
And they were swept to their deaths – AMEN.
What happened to our heroine?
Who knows? Who gives a damn?
She died, it's said, of poison,
Boudica, Superwoman and Mam!

A Fiery Fact

Unfortunately everyone forgot all about Boudica's
exploits until Victoria (Boudica in English) became
queen during the appalling Victorian age. Then suddenly
they began to celebrate her victories and to raise
statutes of her in London and Cardiff. But there aren't
any statues to Suetonius Paulinus are there? So hip hip
hurray to Boudica, incredible queen of the Celts!

Number 4: Arianrhod and her spiteful spells.

Though this woeful woman's tale is told in the legends
of the Mabinogion, it probably does date back to Celtic
times. According to the legend Arianrhod cast a spell
on her own son. She said he would never:

- have a name of his own,
- be able to carry arms,
- and that he would never have a proper wife – never
ever.

[4] Yes, yes, this is the same Suetonius Paulinus as the one who had killed
and slaughtered Anglesey's awesome women.

I don't know my name, I'm not allowed to carry a sword and I haven't got a wife. Boo-hoo!

Don't worry bach – you're only six months' old!

Poor mite.

But the boy had an uncle called Uncle Gwydion who was a marvellous magician. He and the boy went to Arianrhod's fort, dressed as cobblers. While Arianrhod was trying on a new pair of shoes she noticed the boy trying to kill a wren with a sling (killing tiny birds with a sling was a favourite hobby among young Celts).

'Well, well' said Arianrhod, 'that fair-haired boy has skilful hands.'

'Ha! Ha!' said Uncle Gwydion, 'You have given your son a name. He will be called Lleu (after the god of light) Llaw Gyffes (with the skilful hand).' (This is a legend remember so you shouldn't expect it to make much sense!)

A few years later Gwydion and Lleu returned to Arianrhod's fort dressed as poets. During the night, magically, Gwydion conjured up a fleet of war ships. When Arianrhod saw the fleet she gave the ships arms to fight on her behalf against the enemy. And thus, Arianrhod's second spell was broken.

Before long Lleu needed a wife but his mother's spiteful spell didn't allow him to have a wife of flesh and blood. And so, Gwydion conjured up a wife of flowers for him, and she was called Blodeuwedd (clever you – you knew *blodau* was Welsh for flowers!)

Hi, flower!

And that was the end of Arianrhod's spiteful spells. She was the mother from hell! What a legend!

Number 5: Ceridwen the wicked witch. Another mother from hell! And another character from the world of Celtic legends. According to the story Ceridwen had two children – a very pretty daughter called Cleirwy and a son called Morfran, who was ugly as sin. Because he was so ugly Ceridwen cast a spell on him to make him wise and clever. The spell had to be boiled up in a magic cauldron for one year and a day. The first three drops of the mixture would make Morfran wise but if he drank any more of it, he would die.

Gwion, a young servant, was given the task of stirring the mixture. Three boiling drops of liquid fell onto his finger as he stirred. (Ouch!) He put his finger in his mouth.

Suddenly, Gwion was no longer just a servant boy, but a very clever, bright boy. But he knew Ceridwen would be livid when she found out, so he ran away as fast as he could. Soon the wicked witch was snapping at his heels. In order to escape from the wicked witch:

Gwion turned himself into a hare, but Ceridwen changed herself into a greyhound to hunt him.

Then, Gwion turned himself into a fish and jumped into the river. But crafty Ceridwen became an otter to catch him.

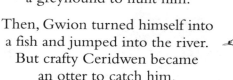

Next, Gwion became a bird and Ceridwen turned herself into a hunting hawk.

And lastly, Gwion turned into corn seed.

But Ceridwen changed into a hen and swallowed him whole!

Mm . . . mm . . . I've had a bellyful now!

Was that the end of Gwion bach, the sinister seed? Read the sequel of this stunning story in next week's crazy comic about the *Quarrelsome Celts*.

I wonder which woeful woman had the highest marks. And why?

CARADOG, THE COOLEST CELT

I'm sure you've noticed how the Rapacious Romans are creeping more and more into this horrible history of the Quarrelsome Celts. And how they were becoming more and more rapacious, stealing the Celts' lands and goods. And how did the Celts react? By becoming more and more quarrelsome of course!

The story of one of those Quarrelsome Celts, Caradog, the Coolest Celt, would have been a fabulous favourite in the exciting comics of the time. Enjoy reading all about him!

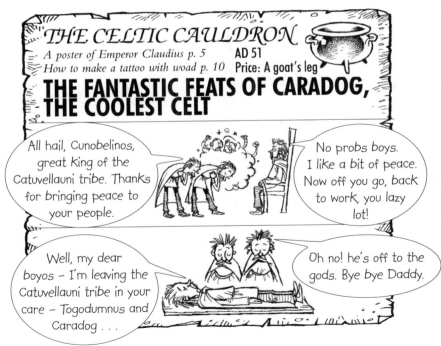

73

I'm Caradog, the Coolest of all the Celts. Before you hang me, may I ask you one little question, Oh Avaricious Emperor? (NOT a good move – he's sure to be hanged now for being so cheeky.) Why do you want the Celts' miserable mud huts when you have such beautiful buildings here, in Rome? (Excellent tactics – licking the Emperor's boots [or sandals] always works). I was only trying to defend my lands. Boo hoo!

A good question and a better answer. I don't want the Celts' miserable mud huts – eugh, of course I don't! BUT I want everyone throughout the world to know that I am the Emperor of the great Roman Empire – no-one can challenge me. It's obvious that hanging and sending you to your gods is too good for you, Caratacus, so I'm going to send you and your nice little family to live by the Mediterranean sea. Off with him!

(Caratacus is the Latin for Caradog: Caradog the Celt had to learn Latin now or he wouldn't be able to buy lovely Italian ice cream.)

COME TO ITALY –
A HOME FROM HOME
(EVEN FOR CELTS!)

Well, well, Italy's pretty. We should have come out here on holiday before now. Even these sand castles are better than the Celts' poor mud huts.

Pardon Dad? – can you speak Latin with us from now on, si tibi placet? (That's 'please' to you and me.)

And that's it – a tragic end to the tragic tale of Caradog the Coolest Celt.

I hope you didn't cry too much when you were reading it. After all, Caradog didn't cry much after settling down in Italy to enjoy *La Dolce Vita* (Italian [or today's Latin] for the Good Life).

A CLEVER QUIZ ABOUT THE RAPACIOUS ROMANS

I. *Why did the Rapacious Romans come to Britain?*
  (i) To steal Wales' best football players to play for A.C. Milan or Roma.
  (ii) To watch Italy play rugby against Wales.
  (iii) To buy slaves – shame on them!

II. *When did the Rapacious Romans cross the channel from Gaul (now France) to Britain?*
  (i) When the tide was out.
  (ii) In AD 43, when Claudius was the Roman Emperor.
  (iii) When there wasn't any more land left to conquer in Europe.

Oh no! I don't want to go to the end of the earth.

III. *Why was the mighty Roman army so successful in conquering most of Europe?*
  (i) Because it was organised and disciplined.
  (ii) Because the people living there were gutless cowards. When they saw the mighty Roman army coming they ran away with their tails between their legs.

(iii) Because their enemies were always quarrelling among themselves. Oh no, they weren't! Oh yes, they were!

IV. *What did the Rapacious Romans think of the Celts?*

   (i) They believed that they, as Romans, were far superior to the barbaric Celts.

   (ii) They were scared stiff of the dozy druids.

   (iii) They fancied the woeful Celtic women very much.

ANSWERS

I and (iii) The Celts (so they said) were willing to sell a slave (even their own sons and daughters) for one jug of wine.

But Dad, I've drunk all the wine! Hic!

II and (ii) and (iii) Emperor Claudius's full name was Tiberius Claudius Caesar Augustus Germanicus and when he came to Britain to celebrate the success of his amazing army he brought elephants with him. The Celts had a shocking shock! The elephants had an even greater shock!

III and **(i)** and a little bit of **(iii)** too (according to the Rapacious Romans themselves). Your horrendous History teachers will love this respectable answer. They like well-organised and disciplined pupils. So copy the remarkable Romans and march back to your classroom. Left, Right, Left, Right – or *Sinister-Dexter, Sin-Dex, Sin-Dex* (in Latin – to prove you're a full-blooded Roman).

IV and **(i)** The Romans were big-headed enough to believe that their way of life was much better than everyone else's. **(ii)** Yes they were, and so they killed every dozy druid they could find, and **(iii)** Yes, and it's not surprising because not many women had come to Britain with the Roman army. Even the woeful Celtic women were better than no women at all!

(* Everyone knows that in fact elephants never forget. Stuff one up your sleeve to help you in your next History test!)

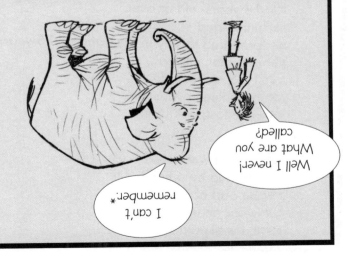

I can't remember.*

Well I never! What are you called?

THE RAPACIOUS ROMANS' AMAZING ARMY

The Quarrelsome Celts' wonderful warriors loved fighting, but they were hopeless at fighting together in a tidy organised army. BUT the Rapacious Romans were extremely well-organised and they were superb soldiers. They would have fought one another to join the amazing army if they had seen an imposing poster like this:

Join the Roman Army
The Second Augustan Legion
NEEDS YOU!

You must be:
- 18 years' old or over
- unmarried
- prepared to stay in the army for 25 years
- a Roman citizen
- 1.75 metres tall
- have keen eyes
- able to speak Latin.

You will:
- see the world
- learn to be a tidy fighter
- be part of a team
- wear an ugly uniform
- be well-paid.

A Tip-top Tip

Your hysterical History teachers will be very jealous of you if you have your own ugly Roman soldier's uniform, especially if you know the Latin names for all its parts and for the soldier's weapons. Learn these terms and YOU will be the star pupil. If you were a real Roman legionary soldier the army would pay for all your gear, but don't expect your History teachers to fork out for yours.

I'm not married, honestly!

25 years: A very long time. Most Roman women died at 40!

Peepo! I spy with my little eye!

See the world: Mm . . . mm . . . you could even come to Wales!

The ugly uniform: As the Rapacious Romans marched into battle (SIN-DEX, SIN-DEX . . .) their ugly uniform would sparkle in the sunshine (in wet Wales?) and it would dazzle and frighten the daylight out of the wonderful Celtic warriors.

Pay: You would earn 1 denarius a day. After working for 150 days (about 5 months) you would be able to afford a fashionable pair of shoes – at last!

PILUM – a javelin to throw at your enemy from as far away as possible (then you could run away)

GALEA – a helmet to protect your head, neck and face (Mammy's pet)

LORICA SEGMENTATA – special armour made of pieces of metal with leather straps to link them together. If one broke – what a mess!

PUGIO – a deadly dagger to stab your enemy – SPLAT!

GLADIUS – a sword to be worn on the right side. But what if you were left-handed?

A neat little apron, not to cook, but to protect your body

A warm woollen tunic to wear under the armour in case it scratches

CALIGAE – strong sandals with nails in their soles to kick your enemy hard. The nails would ring out as you marched – TRAMP, TRAMP, TRAMP and the noise would scare your enemy

SCUTUM – a large rectangular shield to hide behind in battle if it became too fierce (Grandma's pet).

Five Prickly Points about the Rapacious Romans' Amazing Army

1. You're probably very good at mental maths. But the Rapacious Romans were hopeless at it. Everyone knows that a CENTURION was an officer who was in charge of a hundred soldiers or a CENTURIA, because cent means a hundred in Latin. But, no, the Romans had to be different from everyone else. There were only LXXX or 80 legionary soldiers under the cruel centurion's charge in the Roman centuria.

LXXVIII, LXXIX, LXXX – where have the other XX gone?

And here are some more maddening mental maths to test you:

If there were VI centuria in a cohort, how many legionary soldiers would that be? [CCCCLXXX]
If there were X cohorts in a legion, how many legionary soldiers would that be? [MMMMDCCC]
And if there were XXX legions in the whole amazing army, how many legionary soldiers would that be? Give us a clue!

Canny clues:
Here they are: I = 1; V = 5; X = 10; L = 50;
C = 100; D = 500; M = 1000.

Easy-peasy? If not, you obviously need to polish your mental maths skills. Until then, take off your star, put on your dunce's cap and go and stand in the corner.

2. Legionary soldiers were paid in money and in salt. They were probably the salt of the earth and worth their salt. (Ha ha! What a jolly Roman joke!) Ask your teacher how he would like to be paid in salt!

Well, well, I would have thought that teaching History to Year 7 was worth more than this miserable pile of salt!

Take this fact with a good pinch of salt (and pepper and vinegar too).

3. Legionary soldiers were not as stupid as they looked. THEY didn't rush to be first into battle. Oh no – they sent auxiliary soldiers onto the battlefield before them. Then they would be killed or wounded first. These auxiliaries were usually men who had been conquered by the Romans and they were often superb soldiers. Many of them were accurate archers (shooting with bows and arrows, not taking part in the famous radio series, *The Archers*).

When they had been auxiliary soldiers for 25 years in the amazing Roman army, they could become Roman citizens! Just imagine – what an honour!

No, you can't be a full Roman citizen yet. You've only been fighting as an auxiliary in the Roman army for 24½ years.

Top secret: To identify an auxiliary soldier you should examine his shield (but not during a battle of course, or he will kill you). His shield would be oblong, while a legionary soldier's *scutum* was rectangular.

4. Every legion had a standard bearer to carry the emblem of the legion – an eagle on a long pole – into battle. It wasn't a live or a stuffed eagle fortunately, but a bronze, silver or golden one. Usually, the standard bearer was a very brave soldier – well, you had to be brave (or an idiot) to walk in front of the army into battle, holding a pole! And on his head he wore a lion's head to frighten his enemy. The standard bearer was the only member of the army who was allowed to wear an animal skin – very handy in wet wicked Wales.

[True – The BOSS of the Romans was called an Emperor not a king.]

5. The Rapacious Romans had all sorts of weapons as well as swords, spears and arrows to help them win battles. Their war machines were magnificent:

- the **Ballista** – a huge machine to hurl iron darts and spears long distances – to strike the enemy as dead as a Dodo (Hold on – the Dodo wasn't extinct in Roman times!)
- the **Aries** – a long piece of wood shaped like a ram's head on wheels to smash holes in fort doors and walls (BOOM BOOM!)
- and the **Onager** – a colossal catapult to fling rocks and clay balls full of combustible material to set their enemies' homes on fire (FLASH! BANG!).

Felix, the spineless soldier

Even after being accepted into the amazing Roman army, and fitted with an ugly uniform some legionary soldiers were still sad and miserable. Perhaps this is the kind of letter Felix, the spineless soldier, might have written home to his yummy Mummy (*Mater* in Latin) in faraway Rome:

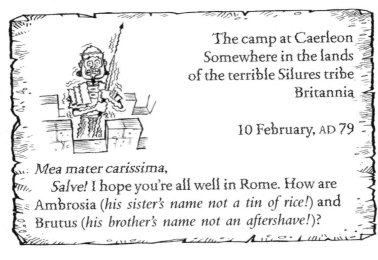

The camp at Caerleon
Somewhere in the lands
of the terrible Silures tribe
Britannia

10 February, AD 79

Mea mater carissima,
Salve! I hope you're all well in Rome. How are Ambrosia (*his sister's name not a tin of rice!*) and Brutus (*his brother's name not an aftershave!*)?

I think about you all the time and I want to come home (*Boo hoo!*). When I joined this amazing army I hadn't realised I couldn't escape from it for 25 years! Twenty five years from now I shall be 43 years' old and very, very, very old. (*You should have read the poster properly, you stupid soldier!*)

Thank you very much for your letter and parcel. Unfortunately the olives had gone off by the time the parcel arrived and their juice had spilled all over your letter. And the eggs had hatched into pheasant chicks on their way over here too.

I hope these eggs are still fresh when Felix bach gets them.

Felix,
Second Legion
Augusta, Caerleon,
Britannia

I wonder whether you could send me socks and a scarf next time? It's SO cold here in Wales. At this present moment I'm on duty on the top of the fort tower and I'm absolutely freezing. My teeth are chattering, my legs are quivering, my ears are ... (*that's quite enough you silly-billy! Remember that you're one of the stupendous soldiers of the amazing Roman army!*) It's so wet and windy here (*an umbrella would have helped the poor creature but they hadn't been invented yet*).

Most of the time I'm shivering in my shoes. And our Centurion is so stupid. He insists that we wear the full Roman soldier's uniform as if we were home in sunny Italy, instead of allowing us to dress in warm trousers and cosy woollen cloaks like the Quarrelsome Celts. We've even got to wear open sandals. But at least we're allowed to stuff pieces of wool between our toes so that we don't get chilblains. The suntan I got when I was home last summer has long gone and I'm as white as a sheet now.

I wonder whether this brown sauce will help give me a suntan?

It's difficult to describe this godforsaken place. Caerleon is on the banks of a big river but up in the hills all around us are the terrible Silures, threatening and terrorising us all the time. I'm so frightened of these quarrelsome Celts. I wear my *bulla* (*a good luck charm – charming!*) around my neck as you told me to, *mea mater carissima* (*that's my dear Mummy in Latin*). But it isn't much use when I come face to face with a warlike warrior, fighting in his all-together (*that means naked*), with tasteless tattoos all over his body. And these barbarians scream and shout in some strange barbaric language Helpus! Helpus! (*that's something like Help! in Latin*).

But thank goodness for one thing. I'm a full-blown legionary soldier now not just a petty apprentice. I don't have to spend every day clearing the drains and toilets in the barracks (*What jolly jobs*). It was difficult to know what to do with the mops the soldiers used to wipe their bottoms – they stank to high heaven. But I won't have to do those terrible tasks any more, because now my job is to guard the fort and to show those Celtic barbarians that WE the Romans are the BOSS.

Tomorrow I shall have another task to fulfil – building a road from Caerleon to the Wild West (*no, no not the M4 but almost as good, and who said West is Best?*). I'll have to remember to put a tent and a frying pan to fry bacon, sausage, mushrooms and egg (*yum, yum . . .*) in my bag. I'll pack some dry biscuits and water too to make healthy porridge (*yuk-puk!*) for breakfast. Personally, I don't think we, as skilful soldiers, should have to do this job. We should force the slaves or some of the surly Silures prisoners to do it.

Every Roman road must *be* as straight as an arrow.

Oops! But they hadn't seen the mountains of Wales when they made that rule!

But at least this work will keep us fit and healthy and the Centurion likes fit soldiers. We've had to learn to swim (*it's a pity the sewage from the barracks' toilets washes down into the river though!*). Legionary soldiers like us are expected to be able to run 36 kilometres in 5 hours. (*O.K. O.K. – it's not a big deal and everyone knows that women who run marathon races today are able to complete 42 kilometres in two and a quarter hours!*)

It will be a real temptation to run away tomorrow and catch the ferry back to France. (*Sorry mate, not on – the ferry hadn't been invented yet either.*) But if I try to do so, the other soldiers will catch me and beat me to death with sticks and stones (*who said sticks and stones don't hurt?*).

But, every Roman road leads to Rome! *Helpus . . .*

Mammy, you can see that I don't like being a soldier. I'm not very brave really.

Oh well, only another 24 years to go before I can leave this army, thank goodness. Perhaps I'll be moved to somewhere warmer soon . . . I've got to go now . . . This cold is making me sleepy . . .

Your darling, spineless son, Feli . . .
(. . . *zzz* . . . *snore snore* . . .)

91

[**A DIRE WARNING**: A legionary soldier caught sleeping on duty would be punished severely. The Centurion would beat him black and blue across his back and arms. He had a special vine-stick for this terrible task.]

And by the way, Felix means 'happy' or 'lucky' in Latin. Did his mum and dad know their darling little Felix at all when they chose this name?

THE RAPACIOUS ROMANS AND THEIR HORRIBLE HABITS

The Quarrelsome Celts had some horrible habits (picking their noses; carrying their enemies' heads around on their belts . . .) but some of the habits of the Rapacious Romans were even horribler (or even more horrible).

I hope you won't be sick when you read all about them. Let's take a walk around:

The Gallery of Horrible Roman Habits

- *Clean your teeth with the best toothpaste in the world:*

Mouse Mould –
made from a mouse's brains.

I don't know where I am. It's a pity they didn't use my tail instead of my brains!

First of all you need to find a mouse with brains. Then, remove the brains, dry them and grind into fine powder. Use a small twig to rub the powder on your teeth. They'll become a lovely shade of grey.

But if you want teeth that are whiter than white, use toothpaste made with pee (a man or a woman's pee will do). Unfortunately this leaves a nasty taste in your mouth – ych-a-fi!

- *Enjoy the company of your fellow-soldiers when you go to the toilet.* You can sit neatly in a row and chat about the weather, the stench or about killing gladiators. Make sure you've got a mop to wipe your bottom. When you've finished, wash it in vinegar so that it can be re-used. Excellent re-cycling – much better than using toilet paper.

And if you men feel the call of nature suddenly when you're out on a jaunt, you can use the pottery jars on every street corner. But what about the women? What were they supposed to do? (Perhaps they weren't allowed out to enjoy themselves?)

- **_Don't worry if you dribble and spit food all over the place when you're in a fantastic feast._** Ask your slaves to wipe up the dreadful drivel and the sickly slime.

  Then tell your slaves to crawl under the banquet table to collect the left-over food on the floor – this will make a nice meal for them.

- **_To foresee the future, visit a wise old soothsayer and take a dead animal (a hedgehog, rabbit or cow will do) with you._** Stand well back when he's cutting the animal in half (**Splat!**) and taking the innards out (**Splash!**). He'll be able to read your future fortune by studying these rotten entrails.

What's going to happen to me? What did the entrails tell you?

This **liver** tells me that you won't be having liver for supper! (Ha! Ha!)

- **_Girls, are you losing your hair or going white?_** (This worried women in the Rapacious Roman Age too, just like today.) We've got the answer.

Tie your slave girl's lovely long hair up with a rope and cut it all off. Make a wig from it. You'll look like a queen in it (or like a slave-girl of course). But the slave-girl will be as bald as a coot, poor thing!

- **Does your best friend sweat and smell?** Does he need help to scrape all the dirt and perspiration off? Then, try rubbing olive oil into his skin. Don't worry if he slips out of your grasp (GASP! Where's he gone?) Then, scrape the olive oil off with a metal scraper (**Ouch!**). (You could use the oil to fry a piece of fish afterwards unless it's too sweaty!)

Stay still! You're as slippery as an eel!

Oh leave off!

- **Soldiers – have you had a nasty injury in battle?** If so, make a model of the limb that's been injured and bring it to the temple to hang up as an offering to the gods, and you'll be cured. (Yes, we know that it was the doctors who rescued and cured you, but the gods always get the thanks. Just like when you've done well in a test and the teachers get all the praise).

I'm all ears now!

- **_Are you on the brink of death?_** If so, make sure you are buried on the roadside outside the fort or town in which you live. (You'll have to die first of course and ask someone who's alive to carry out your wishes). Unless you do so, your ghost will be expected to rise up from its grave to frighten the unfortunate living inhabitants.

- **_Do you want to prove that you really are a Rapacious Roman?_** Then, you must dress like one in a tidy TOGA – the truly splendid dress of every Roman worth his salt. You can make your own toga. Go down to the market and buy a piece of white woollen cloth. You will need about six metres.

  _1_. Put on your best tunic and tie it with a cord around your waist.

  _2_. Wrap the long piece of material around your body. Throw one piece over your left shoulder. There should be lots of folds at the back and make sure that one piece hangs over your left arm. Are you in a massive muddle? Are you in a nasty hole? Then get out of it!

I don't think I've quite got the hang of wearing a toga!

Unfortunately – wearing a tidy toga was a very silly habit if you lived in a windy country like Wales. You would freeze in it. And if the wind blew your toga up, then everyone would see your . . . (Sh . . . sh . . . I can't bear the thought!)

Well, well, I've always wondered what the Romans wore under their togas!

Fortunately – you could wear a SUBLIGACULUM, or warm pants, under your toga to keep your bottom warm.

Very fortunately – the women were wiser than the men – they didn't wear a silly toga. They wore a *stola* – a delightful dress with a belt at its waist.

And very, very fortunately – the women also wore *subligaculum* under their *stolas* in case the wind blew strongly . . .

ONE LAST EVEN HORRIBLER HABIT

- *Are you an inventive vandal who likes to write graffiti on walls (and on class desks)?*
Then you would have made a brilliant Rapacious Roman. They just loved writing all kinds of messy messages on walls. Dress up as a Roman (in a tidy toga) and write your message on the school wall – in Latin, of course. Tell everyone that it's your History homework.

★ Guess who won!

A FABULOUS FEAST WITH THE RAPACIOUS ROMANS

They say that an army marches on its stomach.

How daft! Why can't we use our feet like everyone else?

But I wonder whether you can stomach joining the barmy Roman army in a fantastic feast?

If you can, then dress up in your favourite toga and come by five o'clock in the evening, to the vile villa of Quintus Sextus (silly name – Five Six in English! But don't tell him or you may not have any supper at all). When you arrive make yourself comfortable – lie on your side on cushions on the floor (comfortable?!). You won't need a knife, or a fork or a spoon – your fingers will do. The splendid slaves will bring you a bowl of water to wash your hands.

And here is the Memorable Menu. Don't worry if you throw up after tasting this foul food. Everyone else will do the same. Quintus himself will probably eat and eat, up to the point of bursting. Then, he'll leave the room to throw up. What next? He'll return to the table and gorge himself once more with more and more food – until he has to go out to throw up again and again and . . .YUK! The Rapacious Romans had a peculiar proverb about this horrible habit:

WE EAT TO THROW UP AND WE THROW UP SO THAT WE CAN EAT!

And when you've had a gutful (of the food, not the company) you could take an ostrich leg or a dormouse's nose home with you as a present for your dog. Ask for a doggy bag. The food will be a horrible mess by the time you arrive home.

QUINTUS SEXTUS'S
MEMORABLE MENU

STARTERS
Calves' brains and roses
or
A dodgy stuffed dormouse

MAIN COURSE
Roast ostrich in garum sauce
or
Boiled sow's udder

DESSERT
Rolled honeyed dormouse in poppy seeds

Enough wine to swim in

Yes, this was Italian food in the Rapacious Roman Age – no pizza, no pasta, no spaghetti, no lasagne, no ice cream, no ... (*CONSISTITE!* STOP! – THAT'S QUITE ENOUGH!)

Do you fancy trying some of these ridiculous recipes? Good luck!

A Dodgy Stuffed Dormouse

Interesting Ingredients:
A large jar
Lots of nuts
A dismally thin dormouse
The patience of a saint

Method:
First catch your dormouse. This will be easy in winter because it will be hibernating. Put the dormouse and the nuts in a jar. He'll go nuts for the nuts and grow fatter and fatter. But this can take months – so please be patient. When it is fat enough – kill the dodgy dormouse. Then cut it lengthwise.

Oh no!
I'll have to break this valuable jar to get you out!

To make the stuffing:
Use some pork, cut into small pieces, and dormouse
meat. Add pinecone seeds and asafoetida or devil's dung
(what horrible names for a herb! But it does stink
before it's cooked). Stuff your dodgy dormouse with
this mixture. Use cord to sew the stuffing into the
dormouse's gut.

Cook the dormouse on a tile in a stove until it is ready
(that is, a lovely brown colour with the hairs all
crimped).

Eat and enjoy!

GARUM SAUCE
(a foul favourite with all Rapacious Romans)

You will need:
The entrails of tiny fish
A lot of salt
Plenty of sunshine (a problem in Wales)
Herbs
Lots of patience

Method:
1. Catch and kill your tiny fish. Cut out their
   entrails and soak them in salt.
2. Leave this rotten mixture in the sun for three
   months. Once again you'll have to be very patient!
3. Then, if you can bear the stink, sieve the liquid
   which has gathered on top and add herbs to it
   to taste.

Yum yum? or Yuk?

In order to serve this sauce with roast ostrich you will also need to catch an ostrich. Off you go to Africa. I hope you can run fast because the ostrich is the fastest bird in the world. It can run at 43 miles an hour!

An important end-note to this memorable menu: Try to find out what a sow's udder is. Do you think you'd like to eat it? Pull the udder leg! And take care when you eat the poppy seeds in the honeyed dormouse – they can have very strange effects . . .

Remember you'll need lots and lots of wine to wash this fabulous feast down. Forget the fact that the grapes have been trodden underfoot by the dirty sweaty feet of rotten Roman slaves – they say sweat makes the wine taste even nicer. And if you want to pee after drinking too much – call your slave to bring the chamber pot to the table.

It's quite alright to pee where you are.

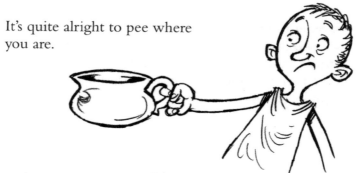

A dangerous drink

A warning about the wine — it was often stored in lead jars. Lead is very, very poisonous and it can make people very ill indeed — stomach ache, headache, ear ache . . . Keep well away from leaden wine!

Fast food

No time to cook? No patience to wait for a dormouse to fatten or fish's entrails to rot? No problem. Go to your fast food shop to buy a kebab or two.

Or, even better, make your own kebab:

• Find a thin twig and stuff pieces of meat and two veg. on it.

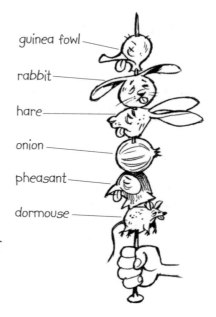

guinea fowl

rabbit

hare

onion

pheasant

dormouse

- Make sure that every animal is dead before you stuff a twig through it or there'll be a lot of squealing and even more blood.
- Cook your kebab over an open fire – Fab-ul-ous!

This will make your teeth water, and then you can drink this water to quench your thirst.

What a pong!

You can blame the Rapacious Romans if there is a putrid pong or a stinking stench in your classroom every afternoon after you've just eaten a lunch of cabbage, onions, garlic, turnips, peas, celery and shallots. They brought these windy vegetables to wicked Wales.

It was the Romans who introduced leeks into Wales. What on earth would we do on St David's Day without leeks? Eat pea soup and wear cabbages probably! And we'd have to sing a silly little ditty like this:

Wear a cabbage in your hat,
And wear it in your heart.

A FUN FESTIVAL OF BLOOD AND GORE

September 23 was the highlight of the year for every loathsome legionary soldier living at Caerleon. On this date the legion, the Second Augusta, celebrated its birthday, and the first thing to do after getting up in the morning was to join the local legionary male voice choir to sing:

Happy birthday to you,
Happy birthday to you,
Happy birthday dear Second Augusta,
Happy birthday to you!
Hip hip hurray! Agi agi agi! Oi Oi Oi!

And then they would all flock to the great amphitheatre to enjoy a fun festival of blood and gore (Three cheers for the festival!).

Perhaps each loathsome legionary soldier would receive a programme like this:

SECOND LEGION AUGUSTA'S BIRTHDAY PARTY

23 September AD 93

A SPLENDID SHOW

of exquisite entertainment
in Caerleon's new Amphitheatre

- Military Exercises
- Executions
- Persecuting Christians
- Wild Animal Show
- Gladiatorial Contest

There will also be ample opportunity to bet and gamble, to eat and drink.

FREE ENTRY

Military exercises

A wonderful opportunity for the loathsome legionary soldiers to show off the latest fighting techniques – fighting with swords and spears, and using their shields correctly unless they want to be killed. (**SBLAT-TAT**!) Then marching back and fore and fore and back in the arena until they are absolutely shattered.

Executions

The Rapacious Romans enjoyed executing vile villains in horrific ways.

Today three villains are being executed:

1. A slave (don't worry about his name)

Crime: running away from his master to join the Celts. (Hey! Fair play – he was one of the Silures and he just wanted to go home to Mammy and Daddy!)

Punishment: To be crucified: that is, nailing a person on to a cross by his feet and hands – a very painful punishment which was meted out to the most insignificant people and especially to slaves. But . . . because those being crucified took rather too long to die in the arena on a holiday like this, and because watching it was like watching paint dry – this poor

Celtic slave had already been whipped and flogged until almost dead, before he was brought into the arena at all.

The Loathsome Legionary Soldiers' Verdict: Excellent – a stunning spectacle and a brilliant punishment for a vile villain.

2. Severus Victus, the lamentable legionary soldier

Crime: Helping an enemy of the Roman Empire to escape (tut tut!).

Punishment: To appear before the fort's court in the basilica. Here a jury has listened to the case and come to a decision. Every member of the jury has one clay tablet each (don't swallow it!). On one side of the tablet the letter *C* for *CONDEMNIO* (I condemn in Latin) appears. On the other side, the letter *A* for *ABSOLVO* (I set free). Every member of the jury has to decide which letter to choose and to rub out the other one.

I'm not sure which to choose A for APPLE or C for CAT!

Come along – this prisoner's life depends upon your decision!

Then, they place the tablets in a large jar and the court chairman counts them:

Severus Victus:
XIII A ABSOLVO and XV C CONDEMNIO!
GUILTY!! And so – OFF WITH HIS HEAD!

The Loathsome Legionary Soldiers' Verdict:
(huge cheers) – that'll teach the treacherous traitor a lesson!

3. Petra Maximilia, a Roman woman

Crime: Stealing another woman's husband.

Punishment: To strip her of her clothes, place a long fork under her chin so that she is forced to stand on her feet the whole time, and so that she cannot kneel. Flog her to death.

The Loathsome Legionary Soldiers' Verdict:
A spectacular show! Serve her right, the shameful show off!

After a marvellous morning enjoying this exquisite entertainment, you will need a short break before the scintillating afternoon session. A chance to have a bet or two (or three . . .) on which gladiator will win the contest and which animal will be victorious in the wild animal show. And to have a kebab to eat and a jar of wine to drink (lovely!).

And then a visit to the toilet for a quick gossip before returning to your seat in the great amphitheatre for the second half of the sensational show.

I bet we've drunk all the wine!

What makes you think so? Hic Hic!

Persecuting Christians

This was a happy hobby among Rapacious Romans in Rome during this period. But the fashion for killing and murdering Christians hadn't reached Wales yet. To be honest, there weren't any Christians in Wales yet nor in Caerleon, so it was rather difficult to persecute them.

The Loathsome Legionary Soldiers' Verdict: They were NOT happy when they heard this bad news.

No crucifixions, no executions, no flogging or whipping of Christians – NOTHING. How disappointing!

(***An awful end-note***: If these legionary soldiers had lived 200 years later they would have witnessed two Christians, called Aaron and Julius, being martyred in style in Caerleon. But of course, by then, they would have been over 300 years old themselves, and probably too old and feeble, to enjoy the cruel sport of persecuting Christians.)

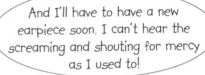

 ## Wild Animal Show

One of the highlights of the Festival of Fun.
Two hours of sheer pleasure, watching:

◆ A wolf fighting against an elephant
◆ A wild horse fighting against a bull
◆ A wild boar fighting against five antelopes.

Then, the winners from these contests would challenge one another, until there was only ONE victorious victor. Which animal would win the contest do you think?

A Clever Clue: The legionary soldiers ate wolf, elephant, wild horse, wild boar and antelope meat for dinner for months after this contest (yum . . . yum). What a feast of blood and gore.

Take that you high-and-mighty elephant!

Ouch! Oh no, I thought I was coming on holiday to Wales to get away from the African heat. This is unfair!

But the poor old bull had been so badly injured through fighting one contest after the other, its meat wasn't fit to be eaten at all.

What fun and games – hee hee!

Gladiatorial Contest

The CLIMAX of the show. A chance to see the champion of champions fighting one another, not for the World Cup or at Wimbledon, but to decide between **LIFE** and **DEATH**!

You will need:
◆ A clean arena – the bloody bodies and pongy poos of all the wild animals must be cleared away (another job for the slaves)

- ◆ A brave referee to umpire the contest
- ◆ Two ghastly gladiators who will fight to the bitter end. They will have practised hard, been fed the best diet (no cabbage or turnips to give them wind) and the best doctors will have looked after their health. And here they are:

Crassus the Gladiator from Moridunum*

A slave who believes (believe it or not!) that he will become a free man if he wins this crazy contest. He's won XX contests already.

Gaius the Gladiator from Isca Silurum**

He's volunteered to be a gladiator (is he mad?) and he hopes to become famous for being a phenomenal fighter. He has also won XX contests already.

[By the way Gladys the Gladiator (yes, yes, women could also become gladiators) can't take part in the contest today, unfortunately – she's got a hair appointment.]

---

* This was the Latin name for Carmarthen. *West is Best*?
** This was the Latin name for Caerleon. *East is Best*?

Dash! I've missed my chance of being mauled to death by a wolf or wild boar today!

Oh dear! You must *be* glad, Gladys!

◆ Splendid uniforms for them – iron helmets, iron masks, iron pads to protect their knees, arms and right shoulders and iron swords (the *gladiator's gladius*). Thanks goodness this was the Iron Age (not the Jelly Age!).

◆ An arena full of loathsome legionary soldiers who love blood and gore, each one wearing the colours of his favourite gladiator.

Fellow-Romans, lend me your ears (the silly Roman way of asking you to listen – so please don't cut your ears off). Today, in the red corner, we have Crassus from Moridunum (BOO! BOO!) who will fight against Gaius the gladiator from Isca Silurum (Hurray! Hurray!) in the blue corner.

The sponsor of the show is Meridius from Venta Silurum and HE will decide what will become of the losing gladiator. Therefore, gladiators – pick up your weapons. Let the contest begin!

The Crazy Contest

Oh!

SPLAT!

Ah!

WHAM!

Gaius strikes Crassus with his sword on the back of his knees (**Ouch!**) – he falls to the ground (Come on boyo bach!).

Crassus hits back and stabs Gaius under his arm. Blood spurts out over the loathsome (spotty) legionary soldiers in the front seats.

But Gaius fights back and **WHAM** – with one last mighty blow he strikes Crassus on his head until his skull splits open and his brains lie on the ground. He's almost stone dead (very, very sad).

GAIUS OF ISCA SILURUM, in the blue corner, is the winner!

Now, Meridius, the sponsor, must decide what to do with Crassus, the bloody gladiator.

Since Crassus of Moridunum couldn't keep his head – we have no choice – **OFF WITH HIS HEAD!**

Meridius: Gaius, congratulations and jubilations for being victorious and since you are retiring from being a gladiator after this crazy contest here is your prize – a wooden sword.

Gaius: Thanks a bunch Meridius. It'll be very handy for . . . mm . . . mm . . . playing in the garden?

The Loathsome Legionary Soldiers' Verdict on the Gladiators' Crazy Contest: Brilliantly gory – with plenty of blood and guts.

A Wacky Warning: Don't allow your Horrendous History teachers (the History not the teachers) to persuade you into taking part in a Living History show like this in a Roman amphitheatre. Keep a cool head and say 'No thank you' politely.

Staggering statistics about the amazing Rapacious Roman amphitheatres:

The largest amphitheatre in the Roman world was the Colloseum in Rome itself (no, not the stunning cinema in Aberdare). It could hold a crowd of 87,000, a little fewer than Wembley and 15,000 more than the Millennium Stadium in Cardiff.

To celebrate the opening of the Colloseum in AD 81 they held a 100 day fun festival. During the 'celebrations' 9,000 wild animals were killed in spectacular shows. What fun!

In a similar festival in AD 240 2,000 gladiators, 70 lions, 40 wild horses, 30 elephants, 30 leopards, 20 wild donkeys, 19 giraffes, 10 antelopes, 10 hyenas, 10 tigers, 1 hippopotamus and 1 rhinoceros were killed. What fantastic fun!

The animals went in tens upon tens, Hurrah! Hurrah!
The animals went in tens upon tens, Hurrah! Hurrah!
The animals went in tens upon tens –
    the antelopes and the elephants,
They all went to the theatre, for to be slaughtered there.
Hurrah! Hurrah!

The amphitheatre in Caerleon could accommodate a crowd of about 6,000 spectators – a whole legion + another M. So the best time to attack the fort would have been on September 23, on the fort's happy birthday. The soldiers would have been too busy enjoying themselves, revelling and drinking, to worry about defending the walls. (Why didn't the Quarrelsome Celts think of this intelligent tactic?)

TIME TO RELAX WITH THE RAPACIOUS ROMANS

It's obvious that the Rapacious Romans had a lot of fun and games in their amazing amphitheatres. But what else did they do in their leisure time?

Which of these answers are **CORRECT** and which are **INCORRECT**? YOU decide!

I. *Where did the loathsome legionary soldier go after work in Caerleon?*
   (A)   to the Leisure Centre to relax
   (B)   out of the fort to see his girlfriend
   (C)   on the bus to Cardiff to shop.

Perhaps the roads we build are brilliant, but the buses are still late!

II. *What would you find in a Roman Leisure Centre?*
   (A)   a tenpin bowling alley
   (B)   a yard and a gymnasium
   (C)   luxurious baths for men and women.

III. *What kind of facilities would you find in the baths?*
  - (A) tingling cold water
  - (B) a lovely changing room
  - (C) a number of different baths
  - (D) a massage room.

IV. *What noises would you have heard in the baths?*
  - (A) sausage sellers shouting for customers
  - (B) people screaming as their hairs were removed
  - (C) people talking, chatting, gossiping, nattering and just yak-yakking
  - (D) gambling and betting.

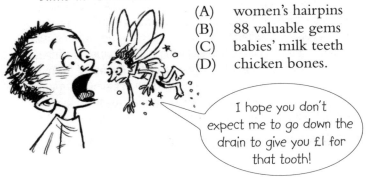

V. *What have archaeologists found in the drains in the baths at Caerleon?*
  - (A) women's hairpins
  - (B) 88 valuable gems
  - (C) babies' milk teeth
  - (D) chicken bones.

(Remember if you decide to become an archaeologist you'll spend a lot of your time down dirty drains like this.)

VI. *Which god or goddess's temple would you have found in the baths in Caerleon?*
- (A) Flora (the goddess of flowers, not margarine)
- (B) Mars (the god of war not chocolate bars)
- (C) Fortuna (the goddess of good and bad luck, not the German football team in Dusseldorf!)

CORRECT OR INCORRECT? HERE ARE THE ANSWERS:

I. (A) There were baths and all kinds of fantastic facilities, just as in our Leisure Centres today, in every large Roman fort, so that the soldiers could relax in them.

and (B) Since the legionary soldiers were not allowed to marry, many of them had girlfriends living in the *vicus* outside the walls of the fort (KISS, KISS – XXX). If a legionary soldier was moved to fight in another part of the Roman Empire, he had to decide whether to pay for his girlfriend and his children to go with him, or to leave them behind. Of course some women were more than happy to see the backs of their loathsome lovers.

But darling, I don't want to move to Spain with you. I love the weather here in Wales!

II. (B) Keeping fit was important for the Romans; and **(C)**.

III. (B), (C) and **(D)** The facilities in the baths in Caerleon were as good as those today: with a changing room called the *apodyterium* for your clothes; a *frigidarium* of freezing water to give your system a nasty shock; a *tepidarium* – lovely warm water, and a *caldarium* – a very hot bath to give your system another nasty shock. Then you could go for a swim in the *natatio* – the swimming pool. And to cap it all, a slave would give you a massage. Awesome!

(Show off by using these Latin terms when you discuss the Romans in your History lessons. Then, you'll have full marks (C% in Roman numbers) in every test forever and ever . . .)

IV. (A), (B), (C) and **(D)** – the baths were very noisy places.

V. (A), (B), (C) and **(D)**.

VI. (C) Fortuna was the goddess of the temple in Caerleon. Because the Romans bathed naked they were worried stiff that bad luck would strike them down, with no clothes to protect them. Fortuna was supposed to keep bad luck at bay.

Help! Where's Fortuna when you need her most?

125

HELEN OF SEGONTIUM'S SENTIMENTAL STORY

Both the Quarrelsome Celts and the Rapacious Romans would have loved this sentimental story, because in it, a Roman Emperor falls in love with a Celtic princess (reach for your tissues – the tears are flowing already!). It would have made a stunning soap opera.

SCENE 1

The story begins in the year AD 383. By this time General Magnus Maximus (or Macsen Wledig to his Celtic friends) has become famous for his success in conquering the Scots and Picts in Scotland.

ACTUS! AGI!

> Magnus Maximus, you are a brilliant general. You should challenge the Emperor Gratian now and try to become the Emperor of Rome.

(It's always worth licking a general's boots – they're very powerful people).

> Mm . . . what a great idea. Let's cross over to Gaul to fight and defeat Emperor Gratian. Come on hogs*!

* This is how the people of Segontium (or Caernarfon) speak: 'hogs' aren't pigs, but more than one 'hogyn' – boys.

There's that job done. I'm the Emperor of the West now. Let's go out hunting to celebrate!

PARIS

I'm shattered after all that hunting. I'm going to have a nap.

We must be careful that dear Magnus doesn't get sunburnt. Why don't we build a shelter for him with our shields and spears and give him a golden shield as a pillow.

(How sweet!)

I'll sing him a lullaby:
Hush-a-bye Magnus,
Sleep tightly now,
Hush-a-bye, hush,
Your snoring's too loud!
Hush-a-bye Magnus,
Dream a dream sweet;
Hush-a-bye Magnus,
The world's at your feet!

Hello, what's this? I can *see* a beautiful city at the mouth of a river. And there's a huge castle. I'm going to go in.

This is like a dream (*that's what it is, you idiot!*) In the hall of the castle I can *see* two lads dressed in satin clothes with golden-red headbands.

(*Wow! Magnus was obviously a bit of a fashion guru!*)

Oh! Oh! Now I *see* a beautiful woman sitting on a golden-red throne. She's getting up . . . (*Magnus's legs are wobbling like jelly, poor thing*).

Hia Boyo! Come in – yes, no?

She's kissing me **(WHAT A SMACKER! xxx)** I've fallen head over heels in love with her!

But then horses begin to neigh and dogs bark. Magnus wakes up in a fright.

SCENE 2

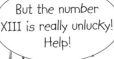

And that is the end of our sentimental story because they both lived happily ever after, Amen.

[Well, not exactly, because our hero, Emperor Magnus Maximus, was killed in battle in AD 388.]

WHAT HAVE THE ROMANS EVER DONE FOR US?

Good question. And here are some excellent answers. Read all about some of the Rapacious Romans' interesting inventions.

(I)   *The Romans were experts at building*
       With concrete and cement – they were stunning!
          They built many bridges
          With beautiful arches,
       Their technology was really breathtaking!

But what can we do with all this cow dung now?

(II)   *But their roads were their crowning delight,*
        They were straight just like arrows in flight,
          From Isca to Nidum,
          Deva to Segontium,
        To go marching and marching – LEFT RIGHT!

Do you know these place names? Isca – Caerleon,
Nidum – Neath; Deva – Chester; and Segontium –
Caernarfon. And back of course!

They built 8,000 miles of roads the length and breadth
of their huge Empire. (They were the M4, E56 and A1
of the Roman Age). In Wales they built a road from the
north to the south (and from the south to the north),
called Sarn Helen, which is 160 miles long, and which
runs all the way from Moridunum (Carmarthen) to
Canovium (Caer-hun) in the county of Conwy.

But remember, if you meet a Roman on the road, that
they always travel on the right hand side. They thought
that travelling on the left was very unlucky. And it was,
of course, if everyone else was travelling on the right.
(BANG! CRASH!)

All right, all right!
I'm trying to keep on
the right side
of you!

(III)   *The Romans enjoyed many hobbies*
          Such as shattering tiles into pieces,
               Then they would glue
               Them back two by two,
          To make beautiful floors for their houses.

Yes, the Romans behaved like infants in nursery and
reception class – they cut up tiles and colourful stones
into tiny pieces and then worked hard to make cute
mosaics from them by gluing the pieces back together
again. What was the point? I haven't a clue! Does it
matter?

(IV)   *It's the fashion in Wales, more and more,*
         To put heating just under the floor,
              But the Romans are claiming
              THEY invented central heating;
         Once more, they were first – what a bore!

The Rapacious Romans didn't have to go down to the cellar themselves to keep the home fires burning, and to heat the water running through the pipes to heat their homes. Guess who had to go down there. The poor slaves, of course.

(V) *We must thank Emperor Julius Caesar,*
     For naming the months in our calendar,
     Twelve months in a year,
     An extra day in leap year,
     He was a remarkable leader.

And Julius Caesar called one month, July, after himself. But the Celts didn't copy everything the Romans did – they called July *Gorffennaf*! Rather a strange name because it means the end (*gorffen*) of summer (*haf*) – in July? Who were they kidding?

(VI) *The Celts borrowed words every day*
      From the Latin to help them to say
      Murus *and* terra,
      Pons, nox *and* fenestra
      So they weren't barbarians, were they?

The Romans called everyone who didn't belong to the Roman Empire and who didn't speak Latin, barbarians. What cheek!

During the 400 years the Rapacious Romans ruled them, the Celts became Britons and Celtic evolved into a Brittonic language. After the Romans went back to Rome, the Britons became Welsh and spoke the Welsh language (Hurray!).

A pathetic puzzle to test you

Can you guess which wonderful words the Welsh language borrowed from the Rapacious Romans' Latin language? (They won't be giving them back of course!) Then try to match them to their English meanings.

Latin	Welsh	English
carus	nos	pain
corpus	poen	land
murus	ystafell	window
aurum	llyfr	bridge
librum	tir	gold
nox	cariad	night
poena	pont	wall
terra	ffenestr	body

stabellum	corff	hospital
hospitium	aur	room
pons	mur	love
fenestra	ysbyty	book

How clever! You don't need clues – they're easy-peasy!

Hey, wait a minute, you haven't mentioned all the interesting inventions of the Rapacious Romans yet. What about our sewage system (hold your nose); our educational system (Yuk! or Bril?); our milestones (Bo-ring), our viaducts (tra-la-la) and our . . .

Shut up – you pompous Roman!

FINIS / THE END OF THE RAPACIOUS ROMANS AND THE QUARRELSOME CELTS

And then, about AD 410, after inventing so many interesting and inspiring things, the Rapacious Romans disappeared from Wales forever. Away went every general and centurion, every standard bearer and legionary soldier – back over the channel along the straight roads – back to Rome. Ta ta!

You would have expected the Quarrelsome Celts to hold a huge party to celebrate and to shout 'Good-bye and good riddance!' But by this time the Quarrelsome Celts had changed and developed, (somehow or other) into bickering Britons and new enemies from Ireland and Europe were threatening their lands now . . . But that's another story.

And so, dear friends, that's the end of our tale,
The curtain has fallen, down comes the veil,

As the great Roman Empire, mighty and strong,
disappears forever. Bye-bye and so long.

We won't shed a tear, we couldn't care less
that the Rapacious Romans were in such a mess.

We won't miss the contests between wild beasts,
Nor the gorging and vomiting in their feasts,

Though we liked relaxing in their baths, 'tis true,
And their comfy toilets for a pee and a poo.

★ ★ ★

But who, do you think, survived all these woes?
The Quarrelsome Celts – those nasty old foes.

And they evolved within centuries
Into Bickering Britons, if you please!

And then they became Welsh, through and through,
And the Welsh language developed too.

And so, we Celts, can shout with good cheer,
'In spite of you all – **WE ARE STILL HERE!**'

If you enjoyed this book by Catrin Stevens in the

Wicked Wales

series, then you might enjoy some of the others
in the series too.

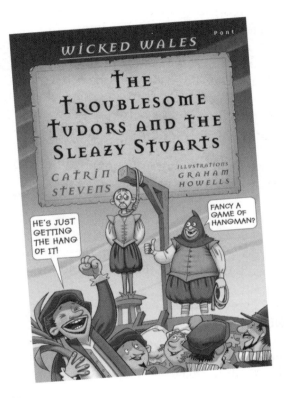

. . . all you need for info on boiling people alive in
oil . . . and husbands who tried to sell their wives
in markets. Read about mad murders and grisly
games . . . and laughable laws! Ha ha!

But if that doesn't sound exciting enough for you,
then what about . . .

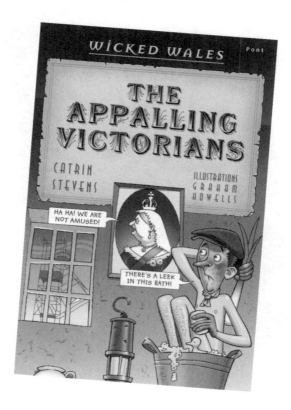

History with a twist? Read this vile volume.
Meet some larger-than-life characters, riotous rebels
and crafty crooks . . .

And if you haven't had enough scandal and riot,
then open the covers of

. . . for terrible tales of calamitous campaigns,
handy heroes and warring women –
and that's just for starters!
Wait till you try the lip-smacking recipes
and funky fashion tips!